Vehicles On The Move

# MIGHTY TANKS

## Paul Challen

🌱 **Crabtree Publishing Company**

www.crabtreebooks.com

# Created by Bobbie Kalman

**Author**
Paul Challen

**Editorial director**
Kathy Middleton

**Project editor**
Paul Challen

**Editor**
Adrianna Morganelli

**Proofreaders**
Rachel Stuckey
Reagan Miller

**Photo research**
Tibor Choleva

**Design**
Tibor Choleva

**Prepress technicians**
Katherine Berti
Margaret Amy Salter

**Production coordinators**
Katherine Berti
Margaret Amy Salter

**Production coordinator**
Margaret Amy Salter

**Consultant**
Clive M. Law

**Illustrations**
All illustrations by Leif Peng

**Photographs**
Shutterstock.com: © Gary Blakeley (front cover); © Zastolskiy Victor Leonidovich (back cover, title page, page 18); © Eldad Yitzhak (pages 14–15); © Dmitry Pistrov (page 19); © M.M. (page 21 inset)
U.S. Defense Imagery: table of contents page; page 4 (JO2(SW) Stacy Young. USN); page 6 (Lance Cpl. Brandyn E.Council); page 7 top left (Steve Catlin); page 7 top right (SPC 4 Long); page 8; page 9 (SGT L.C. Clipper); page 10 (David M. Roth); page 11, 12 (SSGT Lono Kollars); page 13 top (SGT Paul L. Anstine II, USMC); page 13 bottom (SSGT Shane Cuomo, USAF); page 16 (LCpl Kelsey J. Green); page 17 (SGT Kevin S. Abel) pages 20–21 (Spc. Henry); page 22; page 23 (Staff Sergeant Scott Stewart); page 24 (Spc Chase Lee Kincaid); page 25 (Staff Sgt. Masters); page 26–27 (LCPL Kevin C Quihuis jr, USMC); page 27 insets (SGT Paul L. Anstine II, USMC); page 28 bottom (Staff Sgt. M.D. Masters); page 28 top (Earl Albright); page 29; page 30 (Spc. John Crosby); page 31 top (MC1 Brien Aho); page 31 bottom (Lance Cpl. Brandyn E.Council)
Public Domain: page 5

**Library and Archives Canada Cataloguing in Publication**

Challen, Paul, 1967-
        Mighty tanks / Paul Challen.

(Vehicles on the move)
Includes index.
Issued also in an electronic format.
ISBN 978-0-7787-3049-1 (bound).--ISBN 978-0-7787-3063-7 (pbk.)

        1. Tanks (Military science)--Juvenile literature. I. Title. II. Series:
Vehicles on the move

UG446.5.C43 2011        j623.7'4752        C2010-904920-9

**Library of Congress Cataloging-in-Publication Data**

CIP available at Library of Congress

# Crabtree Publishing Company

www.crabtreebooks.com        1-800-387-7650

Printed in the U.S.A./082010/BA20100709

**Published in Canada**
**Crabtree Publishing**
616 Welland Ave.
St. Catharines, ON
L2M 5V6

**Published in the United States**
**Crabtree Publishing**
PMB 59051
350 Fifth Avenue, 59th Floor
New York, New York 10118

**Published in the United Kingdom**
**Crabtree Publishing**
Maritime House
Basin Road North, Hove
BN41 1WR

**Published in Australia**
**Crabtree Publishing**
386 Mt. Alexander Rd.
Ascot Vale (Melbourne)
VIC 3032

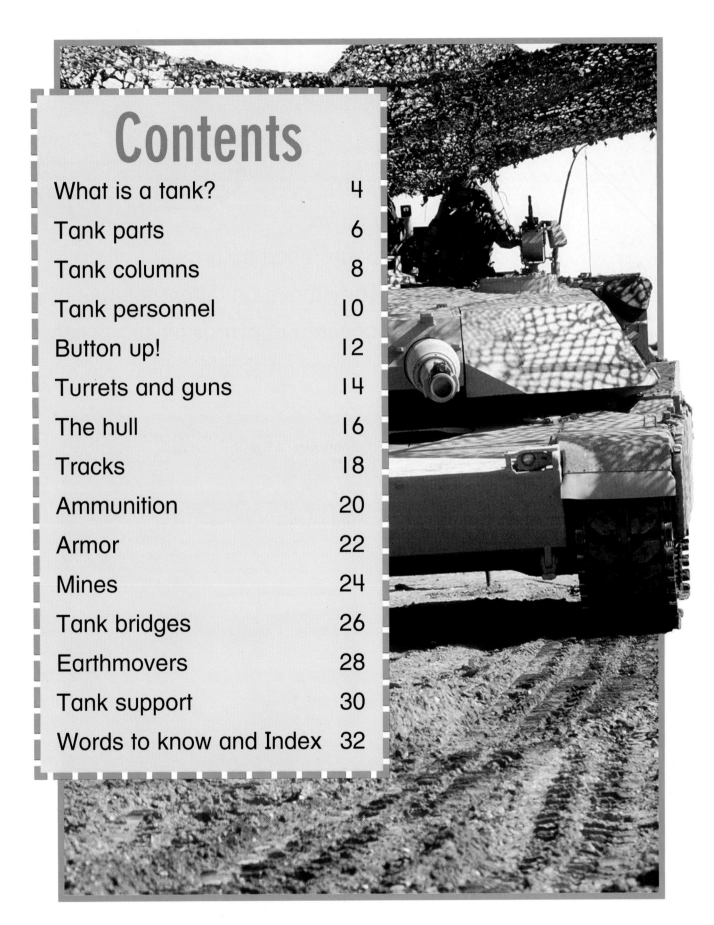

# Contents

# What is a tank?

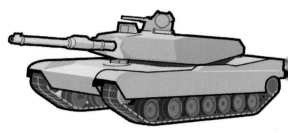

**Tanks** are military fighting **vehicles**. Vehicles are machines that can move and do work. Tanks are used by armies to fight on the front lines. They move on different types of surfaces, and are covered in **armor** for protection. Few battlefield weapons can stop a tank!

*Armies all over the world use tanks. These vehicles can be used on rocky ground, open fields, and in the desert.*

# Why is it called a "tank"?

The modern tank got its name in World War I. The British army was building tanks for battle, and it wanted to keep these plans secret. The military shipped the tanks to France in wooden crates marked "water tanks." Everyone thought that the new vehicles were "tanks" for carrying water!

*The Mark I was the first tank used by the British Army in World War I. It was first used in a battle in France in 1916.*

# Tank parts

Tanks have many parts. Each part does a different job. Almost all tanks have the same main parts. The **hull** is the main body of a tank. Tanks also have guns of different sizes. Guns are mounted in a **turret**. Look at the picture below to learn more!

machine guns

cupola

periscope

turret

hull

armored skirt

drivers hatch

sprocket wheel

track

road wheel

# Camouflage

Tanks are painted in colors that are similar to their surroundings. This **camouflage** helps tanks hide from the enemy on battlefields. Soldiers sometimes even use tree branches and grass to camouflage their tank!

*These military vehicles are painted green to help them blend into the woods around them.*

*Tree branches and grass on top of this tank make it look like a moving bush!*

coaxial gun

main gun

glacis

mine plow attachment

*This tank is painted gray-yellow to blend with desert sand.*

# Tank columns

Tanks usually travel in groups, called **columns**. A group of four tanks forms a **platoon**. Each platoon has a platoon leader. The platoon leader gives orders to a platoon sergeant and tank commanders.

platoon leader

*Tanks move in groups so that each one can support the other. This makes it harder for enemy armies to attack them.*

# Tank crew

In battle, four soldiers
work together in a tank:
a **commander**, a **driver**, a **gunner**,
and a **loader**. They work together to
drive the tank and to operate its controls.

*Each member of a tank crew has special skills and their own jobs to do.*
*Members of the crew have to know what the others are doing at all times.*

# Tank personnel

The tank commander communicates with the other tank commanders in a platoon. The tank commander also gives orders and directs the rest of the crew. The commander chooses what targets the tank is going to aim at and helps select which **ammunition** to use against these targets.

*The loader and commander may also operate the two machine guns mounted on top of the turret.*

The tank gunner operates the turret and fires the main gun. The tank gunner also controls the front machine gun. The loader places the ammunition into the rear of the gun barrel called the **breech.** The loader gets the gun ready to fire. Just like the driver of a car or bus, the tank driver steers and stops the tank.

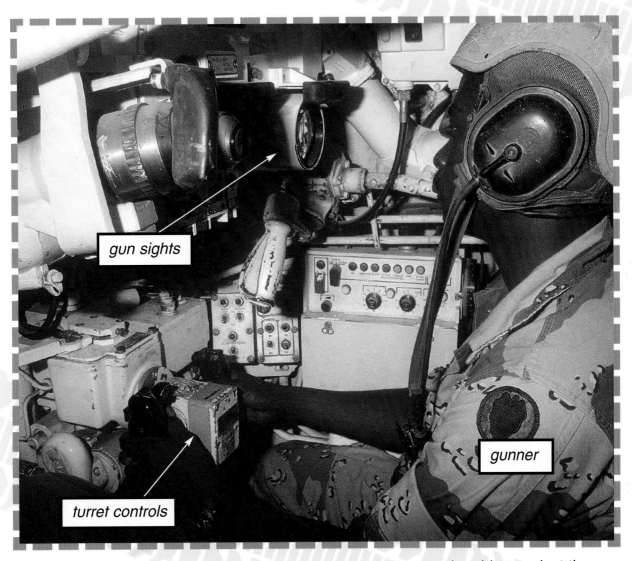

gun sights

turret controls

gunner

*The gunner operates the main gun of a tank. The gunner must be able to select the proper ammunition when shooting at enemy targets.*

# Button up!

When ready for battle, the tank's crew "buttons up" the tank. To do this, they close all the hatches and openings of the tank. This makes the tank safe on the inside. To look outside the tank, the crew uses **periscopes** that peer out through very thick glass.

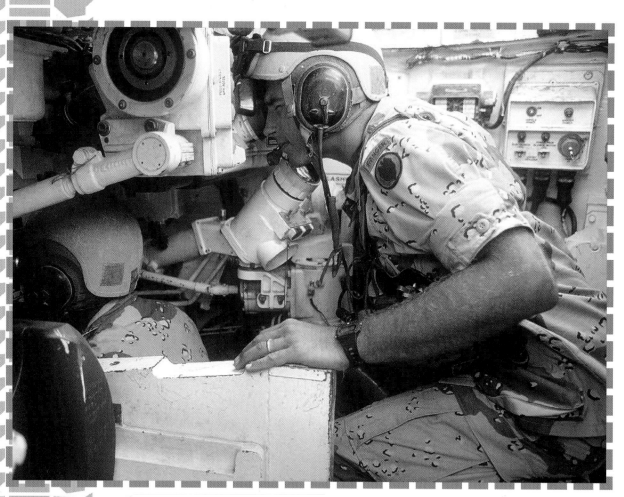

*A tank driver sits below the commander. The commander looks outside the tank through a periscope. There is not a lot of room to work inside a tank!*

# Night vision

Sometimes tanks go into battle at night. Even though it is dark, the crew must still be able to see the things around them. To do this, tank crews use special night vision sensors instead of periscopes. Night vision makes people and vehicles outside the tank appear "lit up" to crew members inside the tank.

*A crew member sets up night vision equipment.*

*With the proper night vision equipment, a tank crew can see a person standing more than 200 yards (183 m) away on a moonless, cloudy night!*

A turret is a small tower made of steel. It is attached to the hull. It can turn and fire in any direction. All of a tank's guns are in its turret. On top of the turret is a smaller turret called the "cupola." It protects the tank commander from enemy fire.

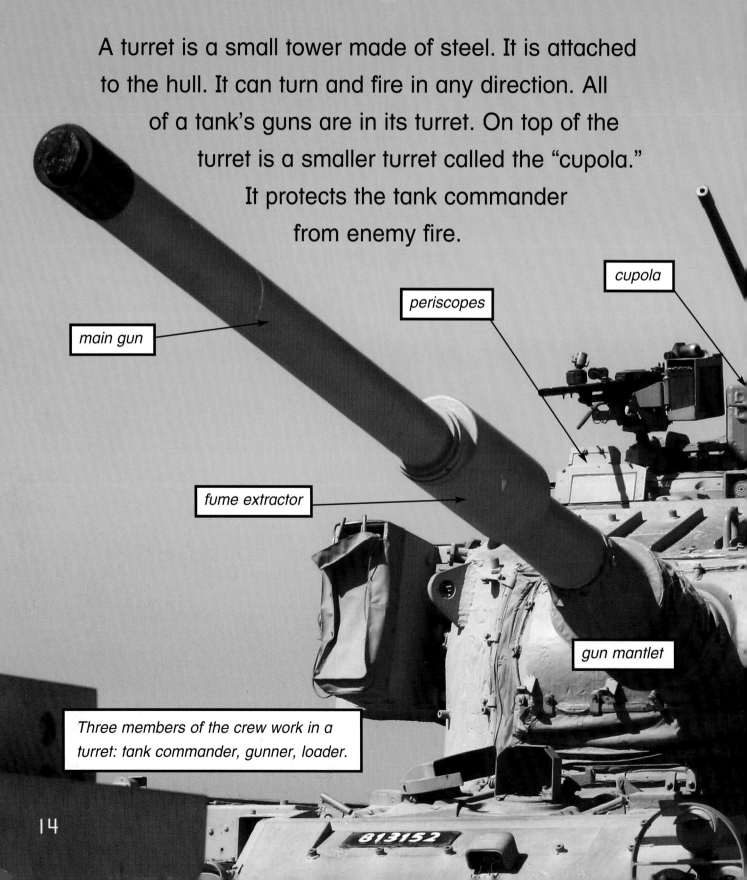

cupola

periscopes

main gun

fume extractor

gun mantlet

Three members of the crew work in a turret: tank commander, gunner, loader.

813152

## Guns

Guns of all sizes fire ammunition from the tank. Main gun size is measured by the size of **shell** it can hold. The main gun fires at big targets like enemy tanks or other combat vehicles. Smaller machine guns aim at closer and smaller targets.

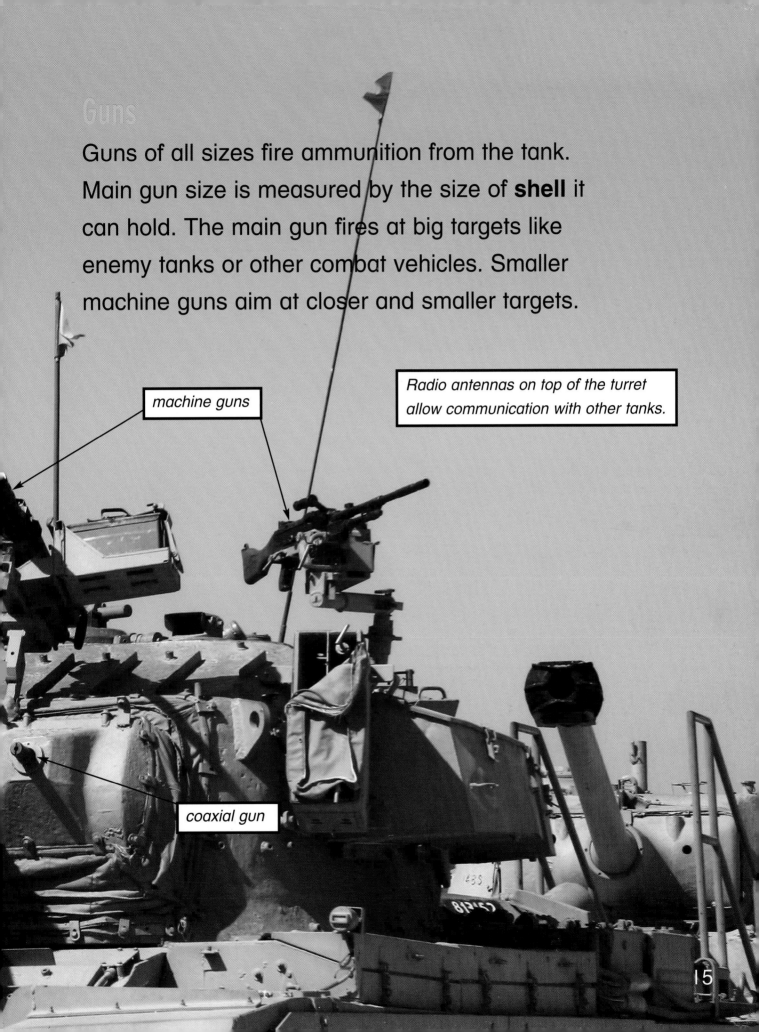

machine guns

Radio antennas on top of the turret allow communication with other tanks.

coaxial gun

# The hull

The hull is where the driver sits. It also holds the tank's engine. The engine must be very powerful because it has to move the heavy tank at high speeds. Its power is measured in horsepower. One horsepower can carry 33,000 pounds (15,000 kg) over one foot (30 cm) in one minute.

*This tank has an engine with a rating of 1,500 horsepower. Even though it is very heavy, this tank can move quickly because of its powerful engine.*

# Driver's seat

The driver sits in the front of the hull under the main gun barrel. When the tank is not buttoned up, the driver can see outside the tank through a small opening. When the tank is buttoned up, the driver sees outside the tank through a periscope.

driver's seat in the hull

T-bar

The driver steers the tank with a T-bar. The T-bar is very similar to bicycle handle bars.

# Tracks

A tank moves on two tracks. Each track has a heavy tread that digs into slippery surfaces. The tread helps the tank move over all kinds of wet and rough ground. There is one tread on each side of the hull. Tracks are built of many track pieces, called "blocks," made of steel and rubber. Track blocks are connected to one another with hinges. They form a loop around the tank's wheels.

*Because tanks use treads, they can never get a flat tire! This makes them very reliable in battle.*

# Sprocket Wheels

At the end of the tank where the engine sits, there are large wheels with metal teeth. These are called "sprocket wheels." These wheels fit into spaces between the track blocks. The sprocket wheels are turned by the engine and move the track blocks like a bicycle chain. The tank's wheels ride along the moving track, and this moves the entire tank.

teeth

a closer look

road wheels

sprocket wheel

track

*The sprocket wheel is the highest one on the left side of this tank. You can see how the "teeth" on this wheel fit into the spaces in the tank's track.*

# Ammunition

A tank needs to carry a lot of ammunition for its guns when it goes into battle. Smaller machine guns need smaller ammunition, called "rounds." Larger guns, like the tank's main gun, need larger ammunition, called "shells."

*This soldier is laying out the ammunition for an M-551 Sheridan light tank.*

shells

## Hi-tech storage

Ammunition is stored in heavily armored storage compartments inside a tank. These compartments prevent the ammunition from destroying the tank if the shells accidentally explode.

main gun

hull

*Tank guns can shoot many different types of shells.*

# Armor

Tanks have very thick steel armor to protect the crew from enemy bullets, shells, and missiles. The strongest armor is up to 11 inches (28 cm) thick. This super-strong armor is made of steel mixed with a special ceramic material welded to it for extra strength.

*Soldiers inside this tank are well protected by the thick armor.*

# Explosive Reactive Armor

Some ammunition is designed to destroy tank armor. To protect against it, some tanks are built with a special armor called Explosive Reactive Armor (ERA). It sits on top of a tank's regular armor like shingles on a roof. When a shell hits the ERA, the armor plates explode. This reduces the energy of the ammunition hitting the tank.

Explosive Reactive Armor plates

The Explosive Reactive Armor (ERA) plates sit on top of this tank on an angle like shingles on a roof.

# Mines

**Mines** are weapons that sit in the ground, just below the surface. When something presses down on a mine, the mine can explode and cause a lot of damage. Some tanks carry special devices called **mine rollers**. Mine rollers clear a path through a field of mines. They press hard on the mines and make them explode in front of the tank.

mine roller

*Mine rollers have a fork that attaches to the front of the tank hull and two rollers that can be lowered in front of the tank's tracks. The rollers make mines explode in front of the tank so that they do not cause damage to the tracks.*

# Mine plows

A **mine plow** is another device that can be mounted on a tank to help it stay safe from mines. The mine plow digs mines up and either tips them over or pushes them outside the tank's track. The mines cannot explode when turned upside down.

land mine

mine plow

*This heavily armored tank is getting ready to lead a group of armed vehicles through a mine field. It has a mine plow attached to the front of the hull, and will keep the vehicles safe from mines.*

# Tank bridges

Ditches, rivers, and other obstacles can make it hard for tanks to move forward. Some tanks are specially designed to allow them to get past these obstacles.

A tank bridge is a folding unit that sits where the turret would normally be. This unit unfolds and creates a bridge. Other tanks can then cross the bridge.

A tank with a bridge unit can move just like a regular tank before the bridge starts to unfold.

Tank bridges unfold from the top of the tank's hull.

When this bridge is laid flat, the ditch will be easy to cross.

# Earthmovers

Many tanks have a dozer blade attached to their hulls. It allows them to break through barriers.

**Armored Combat Earthmovers** are called in when roads need to be built in combat zones. They can also dig spots for tanks to sit, or ditches that make it hard for enemy tanks to advance.

*This Armored Combat Earthmover is working in a desert area.*

*Explosive Reactive Armor plates*

*dozer blade*

*This tank has a dozer blade attached to its hull. The blade allows it to remove obstacles or break through barriers.*

# Armored recovery vehicles

What happens when tanks overturn or need to have parts replaced during a battle? Armored recovery vehicles are called in!

These vehicles are bigger and heavier than tanks. They have huge cranes, and can easily lift tanks that have turned over, or need to be repaired. As well, these cranes can pull tanks out of swamps or muddy areas.

armored recovery vehicle

overturned tank

*The crane on this recovery vehicle can easily put an overturned tank back on track.*

# Tank support

In battle, tanks often need other vehicles to travel with them. One of these is called the Bradley Fighting Vehicle (BFV). This vehicle keeps soldiers safe as it brings them to the battlefield.

Like a tank, the BFV is armed and can defend itself and the soldiers inside. It is also  fast enough to keep up with tanks and can be used as an ambulance.

*The BFV was named for Omar Bradley, a famous American general in World War II. Today, BFVs are often used as transportation for commanders on the battlefield.*

## On land and water

Some BFVs are designed so that their tracks can move them over water as well as land. A vehicle that can move on both land and water is called an **amphibious** vehicle.

*Amphibious vehicles have tracks that can move the vehicle in water.*

amphibious BFV

*Amphibious BFVs can be used in battles on land or in water.*

# Words to know and Index

**tank with dozer blade**
page 28

**mine**
page 24, 25

**shell**
pages 15,
21, 22

**column**
page 8

**tank**
page 4